JUBILEE PARTY

David Carson

## INTRODUCTION

Compounded interest if added to debt, especially governmental debt, causes the debt to explode towards infinity; however someone or something must own the debt. Debt is an asset to the owner; therefore the owner's asset also explodes towards infinity. A financial system built on compound interest must confront the problem of exploding debts and assets. In addition, there are problems inherent in a banking system based on fractional reserve creation of money by individual banks; on top of that the U.S. version of money serves as an international reserve currency. An international reserve currency is valued partially because it is a stable store of value, whereas a sovereign currency like the dollar has value to its home country because it can be inflated and watered according to domestic political problems. Beyond that, the central bank of the U.S., the Federal Reserve, serves as a private middleman skimming money from the U.S. Treasury as part of the Treasury's money printing operations.

The only reasons this rickety and Rube Goldberg structure has lasted this long are the fossil-fueled expansion of global trade and business that can cope with compounded debts, and the adroit frauds of banks on both sides of the Atlantic that are too big to fail or jail. Unfortunately, because of the depletion of cheap fossil fuels for trade and business, these banks are too big to bail also. Continued bailouts and bail-ins of these mammoth banks will lead to serial national bankruptcies. Is it possible to have a bankrupt nation with a solvent banking system, especially if the bankruptcy is caused by the banking system?

## Public Banking

In ancient Mesopotamian valley civilizations and elsewhere in ancient civilizations, the problem with compound interest on debt or assets that eventually destroy both was understood and met with Jubilees or cancellations of debts and the wiping out of their corresponding assets. There are several modern equivalents of the same process, of Jubilees. During the Great Depression of the 1930s, Roosevelt's administration cancelled many of the mortgage debts of unemployed workers. In 1947 the Allied powers cancelled many of the debts that had been incurred by the Nazi regime for Germany. A very small and inconsequential cancellation of mortgage debt was made recently by the Obama administration. The bailout of the banking and financial industries in the West, on the other hand, was not a Jubilee or cancellation of debt. The western countries possessed by their financial companies were forced to print money for their insolvent banks, and to put the bad loans on public ledgers; that is, to assume the bad debts of insolvent banks, insurance companies, and hedge funds. Rather than cancel the debts and assets as in a real Jubilee, the debts and assets were moved to national books, thus threatening entire nations with insolvency also. Many of these nations have responded with wild printing of their fiat currencies. Ben Bernanke, recent head of the central bank of the U.S., was called Helicopter Ben to honor his idea of dumping huge amounts of currency out the doors of helicopters.

The major difference between ancient and modern times in this respect is that in ancient times most debts were owed to the state whereas in modern times private citizens who had purchased their governments generated the debts and who wouldn't jeopardize their positions by granting a Jubilee which would wipe out their assets and privileges. Ancient Jubilees were usually declared when the state changed hands, especially when the new king was not related to the previous king in any way. Although this may appear to be a source of instability, it is actually the opposite since it gives the large class of debtors a fresh start, a reason to hope and to support the state. A Jubilee may contribute much more to a state's stability than various repressive state organs of intelligence and security which must rely on fear and force.

An effective Jubilee demands honesty, integrity, and intelligence. For example, the big banks should not be excused from the debts they owe their depositors in the form of bank deposits. However the banks are edging towards just this kind of Jubilee for themselves by promoting bankruptcy laws that demote bank deposits to junior, uncollateralized debt while elevating debt owed to bondholders and derivative counter parties to senior level. The argument for this arrangement is the existence of insurance for bank depositors in many countries. In the U.S., at least, the deposit insurance fund is very low and could not cover large claims.

An accurate and honest accounting using standards in place before the advent of the kleptocratic Clinton administration, according to John Williams of shadowstats.com, show a declining GDP since the start of the current century and an unemployment rate over 20% since 2009. If the depression during the 1930s was the Great Depression, then the current depression is the Colossal Depression. According to the two factions of the Democratic-Republican Party, the colossal depression doesn't even exist, and the American economy has been in recovery since 2009. Instead of bothering to mention the collapse of the economy and the banking system, the political factions talk about nothing other than gay marriage, feminism, immigration, minority issues, and other carefully constructed divide-and-conquer distractions.

Meanwhile the country cruises towards another financial collapse by using debt as a substitute for income that has been missing since we began to hit the ecological wall and the price of oil doubled several times. Higher education needs a severe pruning and now subsists on student debt that cannot be discharged by the student debtor. Housing is overpriced due to large interest free subsidies to large corporate rentiers who gobble up fleets of houses with cash, corporations goose their stock prices with low interest rate debt for stock buybacks, consumers buy goods on credit, oil companies cover their expenses with debt and outright government subsidies, etc. The entire debt structure requires very low rates of interest for wealthy debtors including governments though poor debtors, the great majority, continue to pay usurious rates to wealthy asset holders who also happen to be debtors in their own right, but on a vast scale.

This stuff is endemic. According to Henry Ford, who has been dead a long time:

"It is well that the people of the nation do not understand our banking and monetary system, for if they did I believe there would be a revolution before tomorrow morning."

Nomi Prins recently published a book called "All The President's Bankers" that should have been called "All The Banker's Presidents". She traces the control of national policy from the time of Woodrow Wilson's new Federal Reserve to the present. Supposedly the Federal Reserve was created to allow the people to control Wall Street, instead of the opposite. The only President who appeared to hold Wall Street at bay was FDR, and only because he was socially one of them, and only because the bankers, unlike today, were willing to admit something was wrong.

The last financial crisis in the current fiat regime encouraged the proliferation and spread of cryptocurrencies such as bitcoin to the point there are over 300 cryptocurrencies now, though bitcoin is by far the largest. Bitcoin is a digital currency, an international currency, which promises a limited issue of 21 million bitcoins, and which is based on a public ledger of all transactions carried on the Internet. There is no regulation of bitcoin exchanges, and the creation and destruction of bitcoins is a murky matter left to mathematical geniuses. In addition there is a Bitcoin Jesus, Roger Ver, and a Bitcoin Bible. The inspiration of all the cryptocurrencies is the failure of the fiat currencies and the failed states and economies that use fiat currencies. Unfortunately, bitcoin has attracted the attention of the suits, the kind of people who might shut down the bitcoin websites if it suited their purposes. At the current time, July 2014, it appears net neutrality will probably be a thing of our rosy, utopian past.

A look at Wikipedia's entry on monetary reform refers to the Bitcoin Jesus, who maintains with great aplomb that it is impossible to block the bitcoin websites. Currently the federal government in Spain passed a "Google Tax" which passes a tax on links to websites onto the old print media as part of a press protection scheme, the U.S. is currently attacking net neutrality, the U.K. has just passed new internet surveillance laws, and of course China is an old hand at blocking websites. Who knows when the laws might require the blocking of all bitcoin sites? In addition, Roger Ver, the Bitcoin Jesus, maintains no more than 21 million bitcoins will ever be created; therefore there will never be a bitcoin debasement or watering. Our experience with past debasements of currencies suggests otherwise. Are the Bitcoin Jesus and his cohorts exempt from a little corruption?

Not to be outdone, the BRICS, Brazil, Russia, India, China, and South Africa, are also getting into the action due to their disgust with the dollar regime of the financial troika, the IMF, World Bank, and Bank of International Settlements. The BRICS are forming an alternate international banking mechanism including a New Development Bank, $50 billion starting capital, and a Contingency Reserve Arrangement with capital of $100 billion. These two institutions are intended to take the place of the World Bank and IMF. Unfortunately this does not seem to be a complete international monetary reform; but only another step in the recent currency wars, which promise to get worse with continued resource depletions, wars, and other social diseases caused by humanity hitting the ecological wall.

One of the problems with our current monetary regime is the failure of international law to cover international bankruptcies, or defaults by sovereign governments. Vulture funds shop the secondary bond market in search of cheap bonds of entities or countries that have defaulted; and then proceed to shop the corrupt judicial markets in the U.S. or the U.K. for a court that will give them a good judgment against the bond issuer. This problem has its counterpart in the widespread domestic creation of odious debt that will never be repaid. The other side of debts that will never be repaid are their corresponding assets, worthless assets. The banking systems in the U.S. and U.K. still use these assets as collateral in their various clever financial schemes and opaque derivatives. Unfortunately, since the assets don't really exist they are no more than phantom collateral, collateral that doesn't really exist. The people who use phantom collateral don't really care since they are primarily interested in lining their own pockets with commissions, bonuses, etc. Any punishment for this behavior falls on the banking corporation as a whole, not on the rich crook.

Therefore, in the construction of jubilee supported monetary reform, odious debt should be of prime concern; and, odious debt should be forgiven first and foremost if not exclusively. Unfortunately the odious debt problem is not simple, there are all kinds of odious debts including debts to or from one of the various criminal clans, debts to predatory lenders on both national and international scales, debts to the World Bank that is trying to usurp and control local infrastructure and resources for wealthy clients, debts with no interest attached that encourage speculation and debilitating bubbles in asset prices, personal debts that reduce the borrower to the status of permanent debt serf or slave. Unfortunately each political jurisdiction has different laws covering debts and bankruptcy in general; and there are widely varying definitions of odious debts.

A lenient enough set of bankruptcy laws could take care of the need for jubilee laws; but this doesn't seem to be the case anywhere since the various central banks, virtually all controlled by private banking interests, are interested in protecting their member banks, not in leniency towards bankrupts or deadbeats. Central banks are also not interested in the kind of honesty and integrity needed to recognize and cancel odious debts. The Federal Reserve of the U.S., for example, is not even interested in an honest accounting of the state of the U.S. economy and lists the unemployment rate as slightly over 6% as of the summer of 2014. According to John Williams of shadowstats.com the unemployment rate has been over 20% since 2009. Williams counts the unemployed in the old manner used before the advent of the Clintons whose support for NAFTA, GATT, etc. helped create millions of unemployed in the U.S. through labor arbitrage with China, Vietnam, and so on. In other words, the employment picture in the U.S. is worse than it was in the Great Depression, while the U.S. has been in official recovery since 2009. Perhaps the U.S. will be in recovery forever.

One of the suggestions for monetary reform include an international bankruptcy court that would adjudicate the nature of debts, odious or not. Unfortunately, under the World Bank, IMF, BIS regime this would probably amount to a form of colonization by bankruptcy. Ellen Brown, an advocate for public banking in the U.S., mentions that several creditors covet Argentina's rich Patagonia. According to Ms. Brown, in 2001 both Time magazine and the New York Times suggested Argentina cede Patagonia to creditors in payment of some of their bad paper. An international bankruptcy court could deliver any debtor country to its creditors, and the problem with sovereign bankruptcies, with entire countries going bankrupt, would be solved. This is obviously a solution dreamed up by bankers without a clue, bankers unaware of the power of militaries, bankers on the nod, bankers with grossly exaggerated opinions of their power.

However, there are other problems with an international bankruptcy court. It's not clear who will be in the dock and who will be sitting in judgment. The bailouts of the financial crisis transferred the bad paper of the large banks and elite rich onto the books of the central banks; or, to put it more clearly, bailouts made entire countries responsible for the bad debts of their elites. Fortunately for the elites, the central banks are either owned by the elite banks or owned by governments that are also owned by the elites. The central problem in the next financial crisis is who will be able to sit in judgment on the other crooks and thieves. It should not be thought that the countries with the least corrupt financial systems will be in judgment necessarily, nor should it be thought that the banking system backed with the most powerful thugs would be in judgment either. In a time of peak everything where entire societies are hitting their ecological walls, it's hard to say exactly what kind of chaos will emerge. Also, one of the problems with any international agency such as a hypothetical international bankruptcy court is the fluid and nebulous nature of international law and the large number of powerful scofflaws.

As pointed out by Ellen Brown, the recent demotion of municipal paper from its former position as a high quality liquid collateral asset by the Federal Reserve, the F.D. I. C. and the Office of the Comptroller is a financial attack on localities and towns within the U.S. The general idea is to offer up all political and economic entities not connected with large Western banks and transnationals to asset stripping in the manner of the recent stripping of Greece. This is an obvious extension of the inverted totalitarianism in the U.S. and Europe in which large corporations and banks dictate to all governments within their complete control. Evidently the idea is to strip all subject governments of all their valuable assets including pension funds, infrastructure, and any other public asset. The corporations will eat the commons entirely.

At one point George Orwell wondered what Americans would do when they discovered capitalism didn't work. It has been nearly seventy years since Orwell's death and there is still no definite answer to this puzzle, although it may be a slide into feudalism accompanied by perpetual war may replace capitalism in North America. Evidently Orwell agreed with Marx who believed capitalism would collapse due to its internal contradictions; though it has to be wondered if Marx or Orwell foresaw central banks destroying capital by widespread counterfeiting and watering of fiat currencies. Orwell's dystopic speculation, 1984, supposed a top down totalitarian regime instead of an inverted totalitarian regime in which business controls governments as in the current United States and parts of Europe. On the other hand, what essential difference is there between inverted totalitarianism and tyranny that is right side up?

The proper international vehicle of inverted totalitarianism appears to be the international trade pact between various large corporations with subsidiaries and business across many countries and several continents. The common trait of these pacts is a non-elected commission functioning to ignore or trump the interests of the various countries involved. Modern trade pacts either supercede or ignore local laws and legal systems. However there seems to be a real legal problem with country bankruptcy or sovereign default. There is no common international bankruptcy law and it still appears possible to get away with an Argentinean or Mexican style default for practically any country. Currently the District Court of southern New York, the personal court of Wall Street, is dealing with this problem by, in the case of the recent Argentinean default, ruling in favor of various vulture fund investors associated with Wall Street. It is doubtful that this ruling is considered wise or useful by anyone other than the vulture fund investors. Favoring vulture funds will probably not set a legal precedent no matter how clever the legal verbiage. Odious debt considerations are ignored in all of this.

The problem with odious debts is only part of the overall social problem since the interests of multinationals generally have very little to do with social welfare of any kind except for the welfare of their stockholders, officers, and, to a far lesser extent, their employees. Certainly the interests of customers of international corporations are entirely beside the point since local governments purchased by these corporations often grant them monopoly powers or positions of one kind or another. Apparently one of the few organizations left to recognize the needs of social welfare are the various nation-states, some of which actually claim to rule for the general welfare of their populations and not for the benefit of international banks and corporations. The various trade pacts are designed to place the interests of the multinationals above the interests of the nation-states. For example, under the proposed North American-European trade pact it might be possible for a European corporation to sue the American government for return of any of its contributions to social security or Medicare funds by reference to the trade pact's restraint of trade clause.

The advance of multinationals through overpowering trade pacts depends not so much on international law and courts, but on whatever military force they can summon.  In the case of North American and Western European multinationals with headquarters in one of the NATO countries multinationals can summon the forces of the United States from one of their hundreds of bases stationed over all the planet.  Although this summons is rarely issued except in the case of Latin America and the Middle East, the implied threat is very real.  However the depletion of resources, especially oil, means the population of the U.S. shoulders burdens that have reduced the bulk of the U.S. population to poverty in order to support their elite's expeditionary military.  Large parts of the social welfare state are missing in the U.S. where medical and educational systems are run by private cartels that use federal and local governments to protect their positions and profits.

However, as Senor Don Quijones says:

"If there is any two-word combination that is guaranteed to strike primal fear into the cold, dark hearts of global senior bankers, it is "odious" + "debt". In international law, odious debt is a legal theory that holds that the national debt incurred by a regime for purposes that do not serve the best interests of the nation shouldn't be enforceable.  Such debts are hence regarded as personal debts of the regime that incurred them and not debts of the state."

Examples include everything from debts incurred by dictators in the name of their nations for their own personal use, or debts incurred by national treasuries to save corrupt and criminal banks. Usually odious debts are associated with pathological attempts to blame the victims; or, as put by a 17th. Century anonymous wag,

> The law locks up the man or woman
> who steals the goose from off the common,
> but lets the greater felon loose
> who steals the common from off the goose.

Odious debts are also associated closely with agglomeration and centralization of power. In the case of the common stolen from off the goose in the 17th Century, the English and Scottish aristocracy consolidated their power both by the use of debts and the enclosure of the commons that led indebted commoners to the desperate voyage and colonization of the Americas. Lord Selkirk, for example, out of the goodness of his heart, purchased land in the Red River valley of the Dakotas to be colonized by his "unwanted extra eaters", a happy phrase coined by that towering intellect, Henry Kissinger. Unfortunately, the main port of entry at that time for the English was Churchill, Manitoba on Hudson Bay and the settlers had to walk many hundreds of miles south through forbidding tundra and taiga to the Dakotas. The future may hold similar disasters for those of us with unpaid debts, enclosed from any city, town or home; and, there is nowhere to go, there is no Red River Valley.

But the question arises, what is debt? Why should it have such awful consequences when manipulated in ways injurious to everyone except a few bankers and politicians? Debt is not quite money, but it's close. Modern banks create money at the same time they create loans; in general, a bank loan is not paper money that comes from a pile of bills held in the bank's vault, but simply a bookkeeping entry creating an asset, or money in the banking account of the borrower, and an offsetting liability for the borrower on the books of the lending bank. Of course any bank is required to keep reserves to cover possible loses on loans, and charges interest on the money it creates out of thin air. The higher the interest, the harder it is for the borrower to pay the money back it owes the bank. In other words, money comes into existence at the same time as debt. Therefore money is backed by debt, debt that will be paid back at some time in the future. If the debt is not paid back; then the bank must write off part of its reserves, in theory, but only in theory. If the bank is big enough and well enough connected it can have a larger bank or government create a bookkeeping entry and buy its bad loan, or bad paper.

In order to cover the interest that accompanies the creation of money a growing economy is essential. Unfortunately the creation of money has become disconnected from anything that might enlarge the economy, small businesses have trouble raising money, startups except in some phony-doughnut technology specialty such as social media are starved of funds, and infrastructure is neglected. In addition, resource depletion from water and soil to minerals and oil has made growth so difficult some governments call inflation growth to solve the growth problem. This is not a real solution in the real world, it is only a phony solution in a fantasy world where hypocrisy is sincerity and lies are truths.

In addition, central banks rig interest rates so that officers of large banks and other well connected individuals in the financial industry have access to loans at extremely low interest rates while everyone else is charged very high rates. This has caused a huge carry trade, which explodes the nominal or cash value of financial assets and blows one bubble after another. Finally, as a result, those well connected to central banks become wealthy enough relative to the rest of the population to buy both the central banks and their governments; and high officials of the government become no more than neoliberal placemen, two dimensional suits mouthing empty slogans manufactured by amoral and unprincipled public relation firms. And ultimately, those who love it most, who love money beyond anything else in the world, will destroy money or currency. Too much money printing or counterfeiting destroys a currency.

Unfortunately, large banks are only part of the problem. Corporations and governments controlled by large banks are able to impose odious debts throughout the world. A whole series of damaging trade pacts assure the interests of banks and corporations come before the interests of any of the local populations. Those corporations that manufacture consumer goods such as Apple are able to export most of their manufacturing to the lowest wage country possible, and then import finished products into Europe and North America. Even though corporations that practice international labor arbitrage generally have no military arm to enforce their depredations, they can depend on the military of their host countries.

In the U.S., congratulations to the brilliant reactionaries who control the Democratic and Republican parties and who have returned the country to the nineteenth century. However, there are actually some differences between now and the nineteenth century, which should be mentioned, just in passing, of course. In the nineteenth century we did not finance a vast prison system bolstered by sixteen secret police agencies and their local copycats. We did not have a huge federal debt that appears to be unpayable. We did not have an immensely expensive standing army stationed all over the planet. But most important of all, we did not face a severe case of resource depletion, a case of peak everything. Our reactionaries are too brilliant and too successful. Instead of returning us to the nineteenth century they are returning us to the Middle Ages if not the Dark Ages.

In Europe, according to Don Quijones at ragingbullshit.com:

"As the real economy (i.e. everything that is not the stock exchange) continues its descent into the abyss, businesses will continue to close down, jobs will continue to vanish at an alarming rate, and taxes will continue to rise. What's more, at a politically expedient moment, the final nail will be driven deep into the coffin of Europe's welfare state system, once the envy of the world. Needless to say, the newly privatized healthcare, education, and pension systems that will take its place will be the sole preserve of the fast-dwindling ranks of the upwardly mobile. Instead of paying for essential public services and utilities such as health care, education, pensions, and infrastructure, the public's ballooning tax burden will be directed toward two purposes: keeping the big banks afloat and sustaining the ever-expanding police-state apparatus that will be needed to keep the collapsing civil society in line. Put simply, we will be forced to finance our own enslavement."

Although Western banks dictate policy to their governments, most Eastern banks appear to be under the control of their governments rather than the other way around. Globally, banks communicate through SWIFT, Society for Worldwide Inter-bank Financial Telecommunications. As of the fall of 2010, SWIFT included over 9000 banks and financial institutions in 209 countries and handled 15 million messages per day. SWIFT sends payment orders between banks that are settled in the correspondent accounts banks have with each other. Therefore, when BNP Paribas used SWIFT to transfer dollars held in Wall Street correspondent banks for their Iranian customers Paribas was fined heavily by American authorities. In September 2013 Der Spiegel reported that the American intelligence agency, NSA, monitors SWIFT transactions. Partially because of American pressure on SWIFT, Russia intends to form its own international inter-bank system by May of 2015, which will add to other arrangements among Russia, China, and other Eurasian and eastern powers.

In addition, China has entered into many currency-swap agreements with governments and central banks all over the world including the hard-pressed central bank of Argentina. China, like Russia, continues to increase its holdings of gold. At the same time, several European countries including Germany and the Netherlands, are trying to repatriate their gold holdings; probably because they fear the collapse of the Western fiat currency regime and want to be in a position to issue their own currencies backed at least partially by national gold reserves. The U.S., which holds most of Germany's gold, said it would take seven years for the Germans to get all their gold back. How's that for strong safekeeping?

Aside from its extremely strong safekeeping standards, the U.S. banking system inspires fear because, at least from the outside, it appears to be a zombie banking system intent on spreading all kinds of zombies wherever it can find a victim. Because it marks to model or fantasy rather than to market, it appears to be insolvent, or already dead. It forecloses on houses and forces their previous owners out and then abandons the resulting zombie ruin to infect the local community; it finances vast stock buybacks which turn productive corporations and companies into zombie shells producing nothing but debt; it finances phony colleges and debt mills that turn the young into debt zombies; it buys armies of zombie politicians that infect both parties and governments at every level so that it can feed at the taxpayers trough forever with impunity.

Although the U.S. banking system may be a zombie system, it is a very strong zombie, a zombie that rules supreme not only in North America but also in large parts of the west and developing world.  This zombie prints zombie money, a fiat currency whose value is maintained by distributing it only to a very few institutions and people.  The amount of zombie money paid for productive work and services is strongly suppressed by global labor arbitrage and expansion of the labor force by including lots of women and immigrants.  In order for labor arbitrage to work, the zombie system enters secretive international "trade" pacts such as NAFTA, GATT, WTO, TPP, TTIP, etc.  It also ensures imports enter North America unimpeded by tariffs or other taxes.  Meanwhile the chosen zombie few borrow money from the central bank or one of its proxies at zero interest while non-zombies either can't borrow at all or pay very high rates.  Prices of commodities are regulated by central bank rigging of future markets in Chicago.  The whole arrangement is tied together and protected from unpleasant disruptions by heavily militarized police, bulging prisons, and total surveillance.

Last night I had another nightmare.  I was charged with depositing four large checks made out to Winston Egg in his bank as soon as possible.  First of all I confronted large lines, next the bank teller told me he was out of deposit slips, and finally told me he would deposit the money himself but couldn't find any account for Winston Egg.  He left me poring over indecipherable computer records looking for Winston Egg's account.  When I finally looked up from the records I found I was locked up alone inside the bank.  This could only be a fiduciary anxiety dream drawn from my experience as a fiduciary.  Unfortunately the fiduciaries at the top of the Western banking system appear to have no anxiety dreams, no twinges of conscience, nothing except robust greed and arrogance.

Shrouds have no pockets; but now shrouds do have pockets for rich folks who set up foundations and other nongovernmental organizations that allow them to project at least a part of themselves into the future. Unfortunately the zombies running our banking, military, and security systems are a prolific breed capable of infecting virtually any social or political system rapidly and turning it into a replica, yet another zombie system. Zombie systems focus on perpetuating the status quo at all costs and in the face of an increasingly harsh reality by strictly limiting what can be thought and therefore, what is politically possible. For example, in the U.S. the abolishment of the C.I.A., abandonment of overseas military bases, substantial increase of interest rates and return to a tax regime, single payer health system, and strong third party are politically impossible because of the threat any substantial reform of this kind poses to well-established elite zombies. The C.I.A. attempts to hide behind American non-governmental foundations in the same way deep state politicians hide behind elected politicians; and thereby infects and destroys those foundations in the manner of a virus taking over the reproductive machinery of a living cell.

In the U.S. there is little essential difference between the two ruling parties; and the voter is faced with a stacked political deck comprised of nothing but three of clubs. The voter can pick any card he wants; but it makes no difference because each card is the three of clubs. He still has a free choice, as long as it's the three of clubs, and still lives in the land of the free and home of the brave. Although it is relatively easy to stack political decks in a winner-takes-all system as in the U.S., it can be done in parliamentary systems too. It appears that the current socialist prime minister of France sees nothing wrong with neoliberal politics; and Tony Blair, the former Labor Party Prime Minister in the U.K., followed diligently in the big footsteps of his predecessor, the Iron Lady. On the other hand, deep state politicians burrowed into bureaucracies, militaries, and intelligence agencies need never lower themselves to electoral politics. Henry Kissinger, or the Dulles brothers for example, were never elected to anything.

One of the problems with a third party such as the Green Party in the U.S. is it attempts to solve all social and political problems in one swoop. The recent Green Party platform in the U.S., for example, was a long catalogue of social and political reforms for everything including banks, the justice system, farming, police, the environment, military, foreign policy, health system, etc. The Libertarian Party has the same kind of platform including all kinds of reforms, and many overlap with the Green Party platform. However, small third parties in the U.S. do not unite in fighting the Republican-Democratic duopoly. In addition, it is difficult for any third party candidate to get on any ballot; and third party candidates are rarely allowed into debates or discussions. In general anyone who belongs to a third party is lumped with independents, the largest voting block in much of the U.S.; and independents can be as independent as they please as long as they vote for either a Republican or a Democrat.  Many republicans or democrats vote on the principle of Least Evil; they must vote for a mainstream politician who is not as evil as his opposing mainstream politician, no matter how bad both are.  In this way the Republicans and Democrats have raced to the bottom where they currently wallow like a bunch of hogs.

What is possible, politically possible?  Peace is impossible because of bipartisan agreement on the good business found in perpetual war backed by great gobs of hogs wallop and fear mongering.  Universal health care is impossible because of bipartisan agreement on the good business found in gouging with a scalpel. Furthering the public good is impossible because of bipartisan agreement on the great business found in cartels and monopolies.  It is amazing the extent our political hogs agree with each other; there are no real fights in the pigpen, only a lot of impressive oinking and creation of phony reforms such as Obamacare and the Dodd-Frank banking fraud.  Any reform is quickly thrown into the mire and transformed into another fraud to keep the mire deep and the hogs happy.

But sooner or later the farmer will no longer have enough corn to feed the hogs, the pig mire will dry up, and the pigsty fences will disappear.  What happens then; or, what should happen then?  First of all, it should be understood that debts that cannot be paid will not be paid.  The real question is: how will the debts that can't be paid not be paid?  This appears ridiculous on the surface.  Currently the debts that can't be paid are simply kicked into the future with various loan extensions designed to save insolvent banks and other lenders, and with the profligate printing of fiat currencies. Central banks have masked the insolvency of their main member banks by absorbing loads of bad paper and issuing many treasuries of various kinds.  The end effect of this is to spread insolvency to entire countries such as Greece, Portugal, Spain, etc.  At the same time the central banks have printed an immense amount of currency allowing a favored few to buy public assets from bankrupt countries and localities for virtually nothing.  A central bank currency is simply printed money depending on its scarcity (except for the favored few) for its value, whereas a locality has to be a tax regime depending on the health of its economy and the prosperity of its members.  Therefore, any locality forced to use a central bank currency is at a tremendous disadvantage if its interests are ignored by its central bank.  Unfortunately, too many central banks are only interested in saving insolvent member banks, and all other interests are ignored.

   Traditionally bad paper is absorbed or written off by its creators, the lenders.  However, the big lenders in much of the developed world have externalized the costs of writing off bad paper by shifting the cost to either their national taxpayers or to the borrowers who are forced to twist in the wind with no or little chance of repayment in a process called "kicking the can down the road".  The big lenders make declarations of bankruptcy very hard for their borrowers; and their control of their governments allow them to shift their costs at least partially to their societies at large.  But this brings up the possibility of entire societies declaring bankruptcy, or insolvency. If an entire nation declares bankruptcy its currency, assuming it has an independent currency, must suffer. Bankruptcies can sometimes take a very long time to happen. The larger the bankrupt, the longer the declaration of bankruptcy can take. The value of a particular currency relative to other currencies might be thought to indicate financial health; but this is not the case. The foreign exchange market is quite different from a lot of markets; it is so large it is hard to regulate or fix. It is also very hard to predict.

As far as big Western lenders are considered, a good borrower is a borrower who can't take bankruptcy such as students with student loans in the U.S. Even though a student dumped into a depression economy has no chance of repaying the money he spent earning his degree in marketing, business administration, art history, sociology, psychology, literature, or any other liberal art or science, he can not take bankruptcy in the U.S. Therefore a U.S. bank can carry the student loan on its books and gouge the student at its leisure forever. Similarly, it makes no difference to Western financiers whether or not war contractors are successful in their foreign adventures. The banks can continue to gouge the taxpayers backing the contractors forever, unless, of course, the group of taxpayers, their country, takes bankruptcy. Currently bankruptcy is still legal for many organizations and individuals from nation-states, corporations, and banks to swindlers and grifters. No doubt the big banks are taking steps to rectify this horrible and unfair situation.

On the other hand, the big banks have made it impossible for themselves to go bankrupt; they are too big to fail essentially because they hold the public's money. They not only hold the public's tax money, they also collect interest and fees through the Federal Reserve on money printed by the national Treasury in the U.S. This is a huge windfall for the private owners of these big banks, a windfall that allows them to control their governments. Their governments and the populations the governments represent exist for the benefit of the banks. The idea that banks exist for the benefit of governments and their populations is considered quaint and old-fashioned in the same manner the U.S. Bill of Rights is considered quaint and old-fashioned by elite members of the legal establishment. The idea that the public should own any bank holding public money is considered a socialistic if not communistic idea that is explicitly outlawed in many of the states of the U.S. This idea threatens bank hegemony and proper social order.

The banking system of the U.S. is especially irresponsible. According to a post on moonofalabama.org, 3/17/2015:

"Especially under the Obama administration the U.S. abused its important role in international finance to further its political pet projects at the cost of other participants in the system. On Washington's insistence the IMF is breaking its rules to finance a civil war in Ukraine. U.S. spying on the SWIFT banking information exchange is used to sanction U.S. enemies by excluding them from the international banking system. Foreign banks get punished with huge fines because they conduct business with countries the U.S. sees as unpalatable. Wall Street's huge mortgage scam and selling of worthless derivatives to foreign entities left the world economy in shambles and investors and whole countries bankrupt but went completely unpunished."

In the U.S. and many other western countries the nation-state is the main backer of banks even though the banks may be controlled by private interests with no particular interest in the long-term survival of their patron state. Unfortunately many of the western nation-states are having serious financial problems. The U.S. was changed from a large American republic into a national security state spending huge amounts on armaments and armies financed through Wall Street banks, and dedicated to the fear and dread of either Communist or Terrorist bogeymen. Although communists and terrorists actually do exist neither one present much of a threat to a large peripheral country like the U.S. Fear mongering of the public is part of the long and big confidence game that has been played on U.S. taxpayers by arms makers, generals, politicians, and assorted imperialists since 1945.

Currently a new level of control or government exists on top of Western nation-states, a series of bilateral investment treaties and arbitration by a very limited number of lawyers specializing in international law. These treaties give corporations the right to sue nation-states whenever corporate profits are threatened by nation-states. A few international lawyers handle the resulting litigation in arbitration. There are no juries, judges, or rights of appeal; and the arbitrations are conducted in private behind closed doors. As a matter of fact, since nation-states are the weak party in these arbitrations, sometimes bilateral investment treaties don't even need to be ratified by the nation-state. After all, ignorance of the highest law, big private money takes all, is no excuse. Perhaps politicians can finally dispense with the painful, hypocritical pretense that they represent the interests of their voters or anyone other than their wealthy owners.

The political philosophy behind secret arbitrations that usually benefit major owners of corporations and banks is "the rule of International Law trumps everything including national or local laws". However, local or national laws are generally passed by parliaments or congresses that in some respect represent the interests of local voters and citizens while International Laws are formed secretly behind closed doors and shoved through ignorant parliaments by very well paid politicians. International Law, as it is used in the various trade treaties such as NAFTA, WTO, TTP, and TTIP supercedes local laws and allows corporate entities to sue sovereign nations for enforcing laws protecting their environments and citizens. Small secret panels behind closed doors hear the resulting suits. In other word, there is really no clear meaning to "International Law" except benefits to the few at the expense of the many, whatever those benefits might be.

Statesmen from the U.S. began most of the trade pacts of various vintages, which is easy to understand from history of the past two hundred years. As the U.S. industrialized beginning in the early 19th century, resistance to conditions in new factories began to increase and reached a peak in 1886 with the celebration of the world's first May Day. Although May Day is currently celebrated all over the world, it is not celebrated in the U.S. and rarely mentioned in the press along with verboten words such as 'socialism'. The end of the American Civil War in 1865 led to new conflicts over wage slavery instead of chattel slavery because wage slavery clashed with the ideal life of yeoman husbandry and handicraft. Between 1886 and 1893 state governors called out their National Guards more than 100 times; and there were frequent massacres of workers such as in Ludlow, Colorado. None of this is common knowledge today, which is only one of the triumphs of capital over labor. However, it was common knowledge in the 19th century. Hermann Melville, the author of Moby Dick, expressed a common sentiment from that time:

"The class of wealthy people are in aggregate such a mob of gilded dunces, that not to be wealthy carries with it a certain distinction and nobility."

Today in the U.S., labor unions and their federations barely exist or only exist as operatives and collaborators of a Democratic Party that specializes in betrayals of their working class constituency. Labor unions are only part of the American thought control and public relations apparatus. Money has become a universal solvent that dissolves medicine, scholarship, national armies, and communities. The only thing that has real meaning is money, the only real crime is poverty, and money grubbing is holy. Wall Street is the American Vatican. Although credit unions and employee owned companies are permitted; they are barely tolerated.  The balances held in credit unions are a very small fraction of Wall Street balances; and the workforces of employee owned firms are quite small.  This is intentional.  Although the foreign policy of the U.S. may be chaotic, the long war against labor is very well ordered.

In addition, the U.S. government is already privatized to a great extent and is hostage to the contractors that act in its name.  These contractors vary widely from transnational corporations of huge size and wealth to mercenary, private military organizations; the nation state in North America has devolved into a corporate state.  The U.S. is no longer a real country; but awaits final dissolution.  The program of the Jubilee Party is modest and limited to offering ideas about the formation of an honest banking system operating as a solid utility owned and operated by public, not private, interests.  We do not presume to know any solutions to wider political and social problems; however, it appears that capitalism may founder on resource depletion instead of proletarian revolution.  Because of the fragility of the remnants of larger polities our attention is drawn to states, provinces, and cities first, although the manner of weaving together coherent banking utilities covering larger political entities also warrants consideration.

Public utilities are common even in the U.S..  Examples are the post office and various electrical, water, and sewage utilities scattered about the country.  Although the U.S. post office is currently under siege by insistence from Congress to fund its pension plans 75 years in advance, and the replacement of permanent unionized employees by temps, no one seems to believe private corporations such as UPS or FedEx could take its place except for the most extreme believers in market magic preaching in the various bastions of plutocracy.  The pension finance law for the post office passed by Congress is yet another example of outrageous corruption by this august body that also passed unconstitutional laws such as the Patriot and Military Authorization Acts.  The post office ran very well as a unionized public utility; and there is no reason banks would not run very well as unionized public utilities.  It would certainly be a sea change.  The banks in the U.S. have been running disasters of one kind or another since their beginning for everyone except our aristocratic plutocrats.

    A unionized public utility is a kind of mutual organization resistant to the kind of corruption currently destroying the rule of law in the U.S.  However, mutual organizations are not immune from corruption.  The Board of Public Utilities in Kansas City Kansas was formed to service branches of large corporations and business located in KCK by their representatives; therefore residential rates were much higher than industrial rates.  This kind of subsidy is very mild compared to current government subsidies to business involving tax holidays, free infrastructure, licenses and permits, etc.  Combined with disappearing funds for general social welfare, and draconian drug law enforcement against the poor, these subsidies are corrupt.  The idea that current businessmen are job creators is not an excuse and is not even relevant, especially since workers are considered a "resource" like any other resource, something to be used, exploited, and thrown away.

The establishment of a Jubilee Organization is not new, although the idea of a political party dedicated to Jubilee may be somewhat novel. Jubilee USA Network has the following policy statement on their website, jubileeusa.org:

"Jubilee USA Network is an alliance of more than 75 US organizations, 400 faith communities, and 500 Jubilee global partners. Jubilee is building an economy that serves, protects, and promotes participation of the most vulnerable. Jubilee has won critical global financial reforms and more than $130 billion in debt relief for the world's poorest people. Our efforts build the political support needed to influence world-wide decisions makers, the White House, Congress, the G20, International Financial Institutions, and the United Nations to promote poverty reduction and move solutions to the international debt crisis. Ultimately we work to create an international financial system that protects and ensures participation of the most vulnerable within the context of human rights. Our advocacy promotes responsible lending and borrowing, increasing debt relief for poor countries, curbing illicit financial flows and corporate tax avoidance, moving forward an international debt resolution process, pushing reforms in international financial institutions, and protecting poor people from predatory financial behavior."

Jubilee USA Network really sounds good; unfortunately it has a lot in common with the efforts of the U.S. in land reform, rights promotions, good governance, and anticorruption campaigns. These campaigns apply to others, to poor benighted foreigners, but certainly not to the U.S. itself. How is it possible to "to create an international financial system that protects and ensures participation of the most vulnerable within the context of human rights" if the U.S. system is loaded with payday lenders and banks that prey on the poor? How is it possible to "promote responsible lending and borrowing" if the entire U.S. consumer economy is based on totally irresponsible lending and borrowing? How is it possible to "curb illicit financial flows and corporate tax avoidance" if no Wall Street bankers are ever punished for promoting both? How is it possible to "move forward on international debt resolution processes" when the last financial crisis was papered over with the creation of mountains of debt and fiat currency? And how is it possible to "protect poor people from predatory financial behavior" when the U.S. regularly attacks its students by forcing them into debt serfdom with no possible release via bankruptcy?

This kind of hyper-hypocrisy is fairly common through out political and social circles in the U.S. However, Rolling Jubilee is quite different:

"Rolling Jubilee is a strike debt project that buys debt for pennies on the dollar, but instead of collecting it, abolishes it. Together we can liberate debtors at random through a campaign of mutual support, good will, and collective refusal. Our latest project, The Debt Collective, aims to build collective power to challenge the way we finance and access basic necessities such as housing, medical care, and education." (rollingjubilee.org).

Their website, rolling-jubilee.org, includes juicy statistics such as "62% of all bankruptcies caused by medical expenses" or "1 in every 7 Americans is being pursued by a debt collector."

Rolling Jubilee, an offshoot of Occupy Wall Street, launched The Debt Collective and Strike Debt to move beyond a debt resistance movement to common action against status quo debt swindlers and con-men. The following is from The Debt Collective website:

"Strike Debt's Rolling Jubilee project has abolished $3,856,866 in private student loans for a little over $100,000.

These debts were held by students who attended Everest College, a predatory for-profit institution in the Corinthian Colleges network. We bought loans from this school in order to focus public attention on the grim consequences of allowing higher education to be used as a vehicle for private profit. The students at this college were conned. They are being left with no good options as the campuses are closed or sold off to other predatory actors. The Department of Education is not doing its job to protect the students. In the short term, we intend to help Corinthian College students pursue their grievances. But our long term goal is to end student debt, along with other forms of predatory lending. Access to vital common goods, like education and healthcare, must be available for free, as they are in almost every other wealthy country. To achieve this goal, debtors need to be able to organize together and collectively use their debts as leverage.

In recent months, we have joined Everest students in their fight against Corinthian and the Department of Education. We've also launched the Debt Collective, a platform for debtors around the country to find each other and fight back. Learn more at debtcollective.org.

The debt purchased by the Rolling Jubilee – almost $4 million worth – belongs to the most extorted students we know of. They were enrolled in Everest College, a predatory for-profit institution that is part of the Corinthian College network (CCI). Now in its death throes, Corinthian is trying to sell off its campuses, along with its own high-interest student loans, so that the swindling can continue under new management. We chose Everest because it is the most blatant con job on the higher ed landscape. But the problems go far beyond the sleazy for-profit sector. It's time for all student debtors to get relief from their crushing burden. That's why this Rolling Jubilee debt buy (one of the last we will make as we get close to spending all of our funds) is also the beginning of the Debt Collective, a long-term organizing project.

**What happened to these student debtors?**

Everest students have been carefully and deliberately led into a debt trap. The promise of job placements was the bait, and the employment stats were doctored. No university, not even an Ivy League college, can guarantee jobs for their recruits nor should they imply they can do so. The goal was simply to trick students into attending, regardless of their circumstances, so that profits could start flowing. They were then set up to max out on federal loans, after which revenue from the college's own private Genesis loans (at 14.8% interest rates on average) kicked in. This formula for extracting interest was reinforced by overcharging-- the cost of some degrees on offer was as much as 15 times higher than the same program at a nearby community college.

**Who set the debt trap?**

*A) The private profiteers.* They range from Jack Massimino, CEO of CCI (who pocketed more than $3 million in compensation last year) to the executives and shareholders of Wells Fargo and Graham Holdings, the company's largest institutional investors. The lucre they extracted from tuition depended solely on CCI's ability to pull student loans from the federal government (a source of up to 90% of revenue) and from cozy arrangements with private lenders. One study of for-profits showed that 41.8 percent of all revenue went to marketing, recruiting, and to profits while only 17.7 percent was spent on actual instruction.

*B) The federal government.* Elected officials allow higher education to be used as a vehicle for private profit. This formula applies to all sectors—public universities, private non-profit colleges, and for-profits. For-profits (which we should call Wall Street's colleges) are the worst defrauders, but in many ways they are just the extreme version of our increasingly bottom-line-driven and debt-dependent higher education system. Nor is the federal government a neutral, non-profiting body. Last year, the federal loan program generated a profit of $51billion for the government. That sum, incidentally, is much higher than Strike Debt's estimate of what it would cost to fund an entirely free public higher education system in the U.S.

*C) The industry lobbyists.* The Association of Private Sector Colleges and Universities–the trade group for the $30 billion industry–is one of the most powerful lobbies on Capitol Hill. A war chest of up to $25 million annually provides lavish fees for lobbyists, many of whom are well-known former members of Congress, to ply lawmakers (or future lobbyists) with campaign funding. Every wheel is well-greased to make sure that the revenue stream is protected. At its peak, CCI was taking in half a billion dollars in Pell Grants, more than the entire University of California system. Overall, one in ten dollars spent on higher education goes to Wall Street, and much of that comes through the for-profit sector."

**The Debt Collective has been much more effective than the Jubilee USA Network since it helped send Corinthian Colleges into bankruptcy and even persuaded the federal Department of Education to excuse the debts of many of the Corinthian students, an unprecedented victory for the debtor class. However, debt slavery in the U.S. is still alive and well if not virulent. It is common for jails in the U.S. to charge their inmates for their cells and meals while working them at wages of less than a dollar a day. Upon release former prisoners face exclusion from most jobs and voting. In other words it is almost impossible for a former convict to earn a living, much less pay back debts incurred while in forced labor. A former prisoner who can not pay back his debt to the ' justice system" has broken his parole and will have to return to jail where he will sink even further into forced debt and labor. Meanwhile**

one out of every seven Americans is currently chased by debt collectors of one kind or another.

At the same time, even Bill Clinton, the instigator of the huge increase in prisoners, admits he may have gone a little too far. In addition, since Colorado and Washington state backed off their marijuana laws, there is a widespread belief the War on Drugs is finally over. Clinton's admission of guilt and limited loosening of severe drugs laws is only another case of "kicking the can down the road." The War on Drugs is an essential pillar of the police state and therefore, cannot be ended. As pointed out by Charles Hugh Smith, the phrase "kicking the can down the road" is the usual description of any policy or non-policy designed to bolster the status quo. The status quo includes the War on Drugs. Although marijuana laws may change, the War on Drugs will continue; or, as they say, beatings will continue till morale improves.

Naturally most of the above is ignored; most Americans don't believe they live in a police state of any kind. In this case ignorance is truly bliss, not that ignorance can't be bliss in other cases also. No one wants to know the exact date and time of their departure from this life, and no one wants to know the exact time and nature of their next personal disaster or tragedy. These are philosophical ignorances for which we are all grateful; however, willful or encouraged ignorances are a different matter altogether. Ignorance is encouraged by the devastation of language with euphemisms such as "entitlements", "collateral damage", "free speech zones", "Homeland Security", "Patriot Act", "surgical strike", and the like. Politicians encourage ignorance also. According to George Carlin:

"The politicians are put there to give you the idea you have freedom of choice. You don't. You have owners."

Of course this is not entirely true since automation, out sourcing, and offshoring has left large parts of the population without owners. Those without owners are "excess eaters" to use Henry Kissinger's felicitous phrase, useful only in the prisons, jails, and the eternal wars.

The radical reforms necessary to avert collapse have virtually no chance of succeeding because the same reforms would destroy the various monopolies and cartels, in particular the banking cartel formed by Wall Street, City of London, and their captive central banks including the Bank of International Settlements, that make collapse into neofeudalism virtually inevitable. The ugly features of neofeudalism are clear, and include rule by those families that control transnational corporations and by rentiers who collect rent on every aspect of a life in which every necessity of life including water, air, food, medicine, and fundamental rights is a commodity. Many of the families wealthy enough to have a "family office", usually families with net worth over 100 million USD, already have dedicated security forces. As neofeudalism deepens, no doubt, the family office security forces will come to be very important and will fight battles between themselves involving whatever weapons are available, including nuclear weapons, since political structures such as nation-states appear to be dying under the onslaught of international cartels and their trade treaties such as NAFTA, TPP, CAFTA, WTO, etc.

Although bankruptcy laws vary wildly between nations, there are always general legal procedures to cope with both personal and corporate bankruptcy. However, according to Michael Hudson, UMKC Economics Professor, there is little or no legal framework for dealing with debts between governments or international agencies:

"Most of all, there is no legal framework for writing down debts owed to the IMF, the European Central Bank, ECB, or to European and American creditor governments. Since the 1960s entire nations have been subjected to austerity and economic shrinkage that makes it less and less possible to extricate themselves from debt. Governments are unforgiving and the IMF and ECB act on behalf of banks and bondholders- and are ideologically capture by anti-labor, anti-government financial warriors."

Further more, according to current junk economics theory accepted by all those who profit most from it, government debts of any size can be paid by, according to Dr. Hudson,

"reducing labor's wages and living standards, plus by selling off a nation's public domain-its land, oil and gas reserves, minerals and water distribution, roads and transport systems, power plants and sewage systems, and public infrastructure of all forms."

To solve these problems Dr. Hudson suggests a declaration reaffirming the rights of sovereign nations, an international forum to adjudicate the ability to pay debts, a law of Fraudulent Conveyance applicable to governments, and the creation of treasuries as national central banks to monetize deficit spending. The idea is to have rational international bankruptcy laws, and banking systems whose first responsibility is to their entire populations rather than to very special private interests as is now the case. This is admirable and well stated. Unfortunately, the very special private interests that now define the status quo, the actors of history, those that define our social and political realities, are busy undermining the nation-state itself with their various trade treaties written by their giant lobby firms. Therefore, any legal or banking structure based on the current nation-state structure is built on a foundation of quicksand.

The current rigging of the financial markets in North America and Europe is a sign of weakness, not strength. Central banks have purchased all kinds of securities in all their respective markets to save their large cartels and banks from bankruptcy and collapse, money is printed in vast quantities and given away interest free to the same cartels and banks while the populations of nation-states that host these parasites are forced to grant these same banks and cartels huge subsidies. It is not clear how much longer any nation-state can force its population to accept this bargain without using the most draconian police state tactics; therefore, the question arises, just how stable is a police state? Recent history suggests police states are not at all stable. Yet central banks can't withdraw their support for their financial markets. Any withdrawal leads to collapse. Therefore western central banks must finally own their entire markets; but, of course, not in the name of their populations, but in the name of the very special interests, the neofeudal interests, that control the central banks. Feudal states, on the other hand, appear to be much more stable than police states.

The current police state in the U.S. depends heavily on the fifth division of the government, the deep state public relations oligarchy. Deep state public relations overshadows the executive, legislative, and judicial branches of government and is only rivaled in power by deep state lobbying firms. Public relations in the U.S. depend on obfuscation, distraction, and most importantly of all, silence. Public relations firms even control the common language. According to John Whitehead, writing at Rutherford.org,

"Clearly the language of freedom is no longer the common tongue spoken by the citizenry and their government. With the government having shifted into a language of force, "we the people" have been reduced to suspects in a surveillance state, criminals in a police state, and enemy combatants in a military empire."

As far as distraction is concerned, public relations control T.V. programming with its endless commentaries on sports by brilliant idiot savants who can drivel on for hours about absolutely nothing. But for anything of importance to the rights and liberties of citizens, silence reigns.

The deep state parts of the U.S. government (the lobbying, public relations, and military-industrial-spy cartels) make rational, peaceful change highly unlikely both on national and international scales. For example, Zhou Xiaochuan's speech of March 29, 2009, reintroducing Keynes idea of a special international currency to balance the international monetary system, fell on deaf ears in the U.S., which relies on the privileges of minting the world's main reserve currency. Many very good ideas for reforms in all areas are dead on arrival in the U.S. because they conflict in some way with the positions and privileges of the deep state elite. The deep state elite must love the status quo, it is their status quo.

On the other hand, Dr. Hudson's prescriptions might work very well for those outside the U.S. system as is now being created by China in Eurasia. Banking as a public utility run by civil servants could work very well in the Eurasian model. However, in the U.S., the various advanced pathologies of the political and social systems make such a public utility highly unlikely except in localized cases. Unfortunately dissonances in laws between various governments within the U.S. make even local public banking virtually impossible. In the state of Missouri, for example, it is illegal for cities to run banks as a public owned utility according to statutes put on Missouri's books during the Depression scare of the 1930s. There is no scare associated with the current depression because no one in any kind of power will admit there is a current depression.

Public banking in the U.S. requires a complete reform of current commercial laws and should begin with a review of everything put on the books by deep state lobbying firms. Much of current law is written by lobbying firms, a public service evidently beyond Congresspersons.

The construction of laws and regulations by lobbying firms working for very special and limited private interests adds to the dissonance and chaos in legal codes at every level; and is a danger to the integrity of any nation-state as large as a standing military composed of mercenaries manning myriad overseas military bases. On top of overly complex legal codes are the international treaties written to benefit various special interests. For example, NAFTA and farm legislation in the U.S. work together to benefit large U.S. farmers at the expense of U.S. taxpayers and Mexican small farmers. Farm legislation subsidizes U.S. grains while NAFTA lowers any barriers or tariffs on imported grain, yet another example of spreading any costs to taxpayers for subsidies to the rich and powerful. On top of both complex legal codes and treaties for the wealthy is the selective enforcement of these codes and treaties. Justice is not blind at all but has the extraordinary power to discern slightest differences in the social and political positions of any subject before it. Of course those at the very top of most societies appear to be above any code or treaty, floating in a heaven of absolute privilege and power.

The enforcement of treaties, for example, is very selective. The Nuclear Nonproliferation Treaty, signed by the U.S., Russia, England, France, etc. nearly half a century ago, was an agreement between states with and without the bomb. The states with the bomb pledged to get rid of theirs if the bombless states would not produce them. Although nearly all bombless states have complied with the treaty, none of the countries with the bomb have complied. This treaty is an empty diplomatic gesture, a cup that is neither half empty nor half full but totally empty, a running sore on the body of international law. Behind this kind of thing is the political philosophy of neoliberalsim, a vacuous word whose meaning changes with time and place, but which seems to currently mean the enshrinement and worship of money and force in politics, law, and society. This philosophy is also common to various criminal organizations around the world that often work together with our current "legitimate" systems.

## In the Beginning

In the beginning there were no central banks, no fossil fuels of any consequence, and electricity was confined to the clouds and kept out of the house and shop. This situation continued up until about 250 years ago until the beginning of the industrial revolution. According to Adrian Kuzminski, the author of The Ecology of Money:

"Most explanations of the industrial revolution, and indeed the rise of the whole modern world, miss the mark. They invoke purported causes such as the development of science, technological innovation, political stability, and the use of fossil fuels, beginning with coal."

"None of these factors, alone or even in combination, provides a plausible explanation. All of them were present at other points in the past, and did not lead to an industrial revolution."

"The ancient world, especially the Greeks, arguably had a scientific revolution, as well as considerable technological innovation, and, under Hellenistic monarchs and later the Romans, political stability, and yet no industrial revolution occurred. The potential for fossil fuels was there as well. China, at various times in its long history, also had the same ingredients; but, again, no industrial revolution occurred. Perhaps also India and the Arab world."

"These conditions again obtained in Britain in the eighteenth century, but this time an industrial revolution did occur."

"What was the difference?"

Kuzminski says the difference was the construction of the modern financial system involving fractional banking, promotion of eternal growth to cover interest on money created by the banks, and the backing of the government of England. Since the world has filled up with people and machines, exponential growth or even any growth is no longer possible. Kuzminski offers seven points:

One. Exponential growth, powered by the financial system, is unsustainable, and doomed to collapse.

Two. The true villain of the piece, and the cause of exponential economic growth, is our current outrageous financial system, defined by the lending of money at usurious and therefore exponential interest rates by a private monopoly backed by the state.

Three. The vast power unleashed by this financial industrial revolution has completely corrupted those who have been able to manipulate and benefit from it, resulting in an inhumane, narcisstic culture of arrogance, contemptuous of traditional, sustainable ways of being.

Four. Our financial system is a relatively recent invention, devised by clever, selfish men for their personal gain. It is not the product of any natural or inevitable process, nor of democratic deliberation. It is a scam. We need not be stuck with it, and the sooner we rid ourselves of it the better.

Five. A sustainable, post-collapse economy on a finite planet will require a return to reciprocal, cooperative arrangements for the exchange of goods and services. Loans will have to be based on current collateral, not on leverage or on speculative exploitation of increasingly non-existent resources.

Six. Usury will have to be prohibited in future lending. The monetary system, by which money is created through lending, cannot be a for-profit monopoly, whether it be private or public.

Seven. Any future financial system will have to be designed to avoid concentrations of financial power, making it possible for it to be held accountable to the public. If money creation is to serve the public, it must be done locally by institutions that are locally controlled.

A more detailed proposal for a future financial system would include a debt jubilee to start it off. The debt jubilee should be restricted to those in poverty who have been loaded with usurious debts that are impossible for them to pay; Mr. Buffet and his peers should have no relief at all. The current insolvent banks should be allowed to fail, and bankruptcies admitted by all insolvent localities, corporations, and government agencies. Money should be issued by local treasuries without any issue of bonds, fractional banking should be abandoned, local banks should charge for their clearing of checks and payments. Local treasuries should advise any remaining national treasury on general policy; the Federal Reserve should be obliterated. Even though the U.S. itself may not declare bankruptcy, a new basis should be found for the world's reserve currency.